RODGERS AND HAMMERSTEIN™

THE SOUND OF MUSIC®

Music by
Richard Rodgers

T0055450

Lyrics by
Oscar Hammerstein II

ISBN 978-0-634-05043-5

WILLIAMSON MUSIC®

A RODGERS AND HAMMERSTEIN COMPANY

www.williamsonmusic.com

EXCLUSIVELY DISTRIBUTED BY

HAL•LEONARD®
CORPORATION

7777 W. BLUEMOUND RD. P.O. BOX 13819 MILWAUKEE, WI 53213

Visit Hal Leonard Online at
www.halleonard.com

CLIMB EV'RY MOUNTAIN

Lyrics by OSCAR HAMMERSTEIN II
Music by RICHARD RODGERS

4

DO-RE-MI

Lyrics by OSCAR HAMMERSTEIN II
Music by RICHARD RODGERS

Moderate Swing

EDELWEISS

Lyrics by OSCAR HAMMERSTEIN II
Music by RICHARD RODGERS

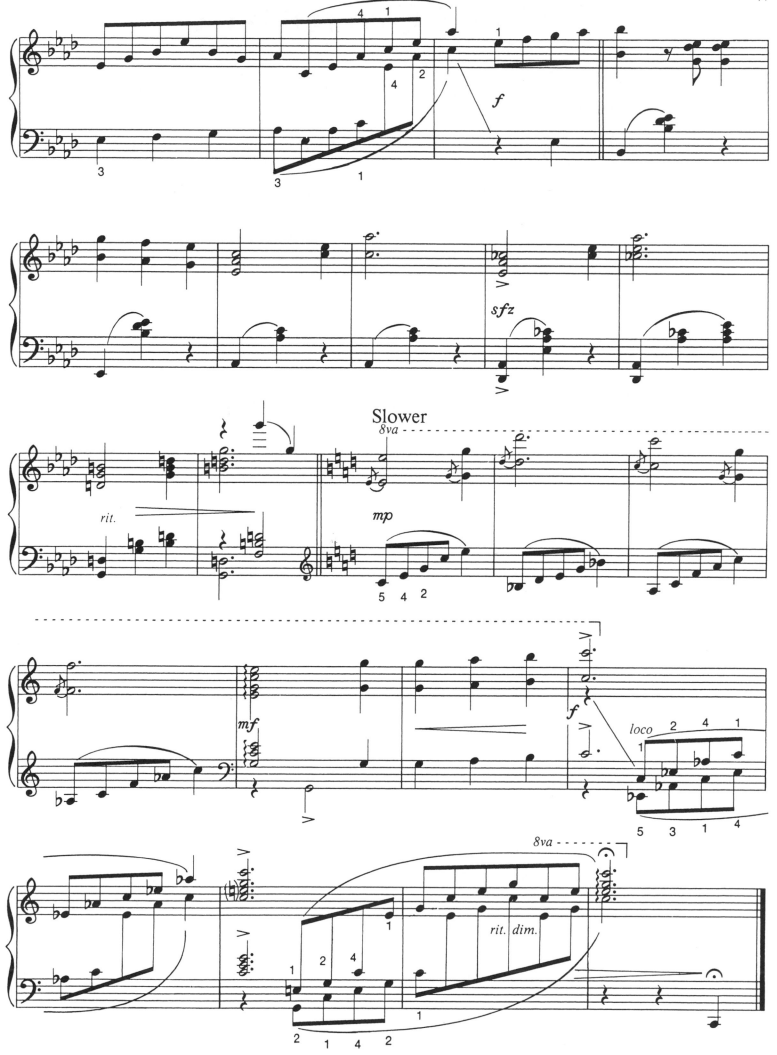

I HAVE CONFIDENCE

Lyrics and Music by
RICHARD RODGERS

Moderately, with motion

THE LONELY GOATHERD

Lyrics by OSCAR HAMMERSTEIN II
Music by RICHARD RODGERS

Brightly, cheerful

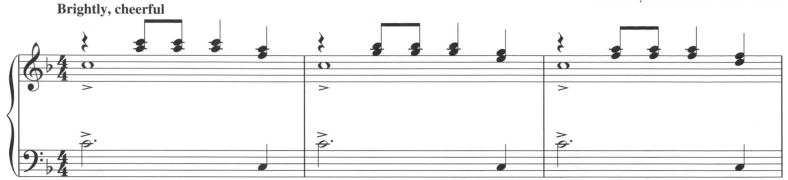

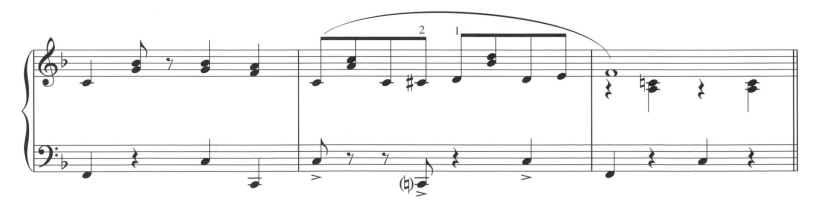

MARIA

Lyrics by OSCAR HAMMERSTEIN II
Music by RICHARD RODGERS

Brightly, with motion (in one)

With pedal

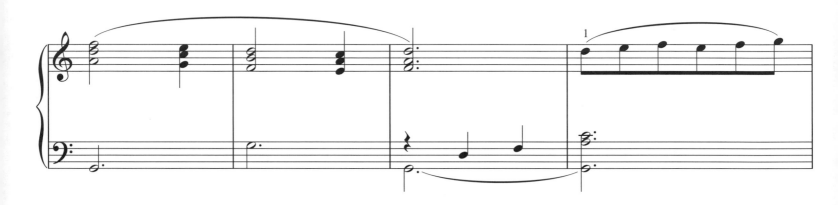

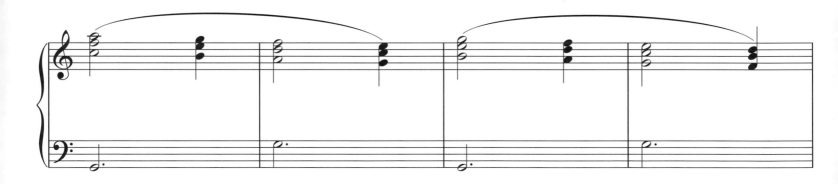

D.S. al Fine

rit.

MY FAVORITE THINGS

Lyrics by OSCAR HAMMERSTEIN II
Music by RICHARD RODGERS

Brightly

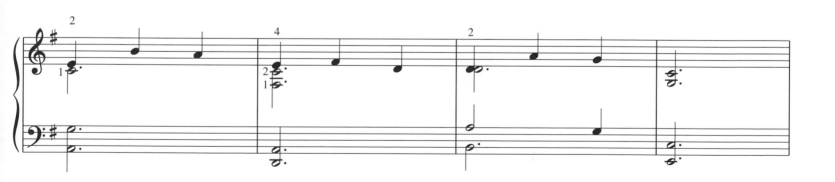

SIXTEEN GOING ON SEVENTEEN

Lyrics by OSCAR HAMMERSTEIN II
Music by RICHARD RODGERS

SO LONG, FAREWELL

Lyrics by OSCAR HAMMERSTEIN II
Music by RICHARD RODGERS

SOMETHING GOOD

Lyrics and Music by
RICHARD RODGERS

WEDDING PROCESSIONAL

Lyrics by OSCAR HAMMERSTEIN II
Music by RICHARD RODGERS

Majestically

42

For the entrance of the Bride

THE SOUND OF MUSIC

Lyrics by OSCAR HAMMERSTEIN II
Music by RICHARD RODGERS